HANNA KROEGER PUBLICATIONS

Aller Baking Recipes

BY HANNA KROEGER

CONTENTS

EGG SUBSTITUTES

 ### Egg Substitute #1

Soak ½ lb. apricots in 2 cups water overnight.

Next morning beat or blend (add water if needed), strain and store in refrigerator.

very time your recipe calls for beaten eggs, take a generous tbsp. of this and blend into our dough.

 ### Egg Substitute #2

To 3 cups cold water add 1 cup ground flax seed.

Bring to a boil stirring constantly.

Boil for 3 min.

Let cool.

Place in the refrigerator in a closed jar.

Whenever your recipe calls for 1 beaten egg, substitute 1 tbsp. of above mixture (for 2 eggs take 2 tbsp. and so on).

ou can make all brands of pancakes, muffins and cookies by substituting this flax seed cipe for eggs.

MILK SUBSTITUTES

w's milk can be replaced by the following recipes. You can use them with cellent results in puddings, cakes, cocoa and milk shakes and you will enjoy ery taste.

 ### Almond Milk #1

Mix in blender 1½ tbsp. blanched almonds and 1 tsp. honey.

Add 1 cup water.

Mix thoroughly.

This is very easily digested.

 ### Almond Milk #2

Stir 1 cup water, 1 tsp. almond butter and 1 tsp. honey.

 ### Pine Nut Milk

Mix in blender 1 cup water, 1 tbsp. pine nuts and 1 tsp. honey.

 ### Sesame Milk

Mix 1 cup water, 1 tsp. sesame purée, 1 tsp. lemon juice and 1 tsp. honey.
(tahini)

✿ Soya Milk

Use a commercial product (Worthington's Soyamel™ is exceptionally fine tasting) or make your own.

Add 7 cups water to 1 cup soybeans.

Soak overnight.

Wash the beans with fresh water and run them through a food grinder.

Add 4 cups fresh water and boil the mush for 20 min, stirring constantly.

Run the mixture through a sieve and add 1 tbsp. raw sugar and a little salt.

Add so much water that the milk has the consistency of cow's milk.

✿ Soya Milk Yogurt

Mix 3 cups water and 1 cup soya milk powder.

Heat until as warm as a baby's formula.

Add 1 tbsp. yogurt, mix thoroughly and keep mixture at equal temperature for 3 hr in a thermos bottle, hot water bath or stove.

Serve with fruit.

✿ Formula for Highly Allergic Infants

Boil 1 tsp. anise seed in 10 oz water for 1 min and strain.

Pour into a liquefier or blender and add 1 oz blanched almonds (about 28), 2 oz carrots, ½ oz red beets and 1 tsp. honey.

Liquefy thoroughly and strain through a cheesecloth.

This formula has all the nutrients a baby needs. The anise seed tea prevents gas and is soothing to the baby.

CEREAL FREE BAKING POWDER

Mix ½ lb. rice or potato starch flour, ½ lb. cream of tartar, 5 oz sodium bicarbonate and 1 oz potash or tartaric acid.

(handwritten annotations: 1c. / 1c. / 2½ oz. / ½ oz.)

Sift ingredients carefully several times and store in closed container.

FLOUR MIXTURE SUGGESTIONS

✿ Flour Mixture #1

For muffins, hot cakes and breads. . .

>   1 lb. oat flour
>   1 lb. potato flour
>   1 lb. barley flour

Mix and keep in closed containers.

✺ Flour Mixture #2

or cookies and pastries . . .

2 c.   1 lb. rice flour

1 ¾ c.   ¾ lb. soy flour

✺ Flour Mixture #3

or cookies and pie crusts . . .

1 lb. millet flour

1 lb. barley flour

1 lb. arrowroot starch

WHEAT FREE DIET

- *Egg substitutes may be used where eggs are indicated (pg. 1).*
- *Milk substitutes may be used where milk is indicated (pg. 1).*
- *Cereal free baking powder is recommended where baking powder is indicated (pg. 2).*
- *You may create a yeast free recipe by using unbleached whole grain flours, aluminum free baking powder, unrefined sugars (or sugar substitutes) and unrefined oils (cold pressed or expeller pressed).*

WHEAT FREE BREADS

✺ Rye Bread #1

To 5 lb. medium rye flour you will need 1½ qt lukewarm water, 2 tbsp. salt and 3 cakes of yeast.

Mix all ingredients and knead until dough makes blisters.

Cover and let rise for 2 hr.

Knead once more and let rise 1 hr.

Fill in baking pans and bake at 350°F for 1 hr.

Decrease heat to 300°F and bake ½ hr longer.

e also Sourdough Bread recipe *below.*

 Rye Bread #2

Soak 2 tbsp. dry yeast in 1 cup tepid water.

Add 2 cups warm milk or soya milk, 2 tsp. salt, 2 to 3 tbsp. brown sugar and 6 cups white or medium rye flour and work this for several min (add more flour if needed).

(Note: rye flour bread has to be worked much more than wheat flour bread.)

Set in warm place to rise.

After about 1 hr, work it into 2 loaves, let rise once more and bake at 400°F for 20 min.

Reduce heat to 300°F and bake until done.

Sourdough Bread

Whenever you want to make another kind of rye bread, try this sourdough bread.
From rye bread recipe above (#1), place about 1 handful of dough aside, press it into a qt size jar and refrigerate.

Moisten sourdough and add to it 2 lb. of medium rye flour.

Make a soft dough with warm water and let stand overnight.

Next morning dissolve 1 cake of yeast in warm water and add 3 more lb. of rye flou to prepared sourdough.

Add 1 tbsp. salt and enough warm water so that dough has the consistency of above recipe.

Let rise twice and bake in bread pans for 2 hr at 325°F.

 ## Banana Bread

Mix 1 cup rice flour, ½ cup soy flour, 2 tbsp. tapioca or potato starch flour and 2 tsp. baking powder.

Preheat oven to 350°F.

Mix in blender or beat thoroughly 2 medium sized ripe bananas, 4 tbsp. oil, ¾ cup sugar, 1 pinch salt and 2 eggs.

Blend mixture into dry ingredients and bake for 1 hr.

Oatmeal Bread

Put 3 cups thickly cooked oatmeal into a mixing bowl.

Add 1 tsp. salt, 2½ tbsp. sugar and 3 tbsp. butter.

Mix 1½ cakes of compressed yeast with ¾ cup lukewarm water and add to mixture

Stir in 5 to 6 cups white rye flour until the dough will not stick to the sides of the bowl.

Knead until elastic, about 10 to 15 min.

Moisten the top of the dough with a little water to prevent a hard crust from formir and set to rise.

When double in bulk, knead again for a few min.

Shape 3 loaves and put in slightly oiled pans.

Let rise to double their bulk and bake in moderate oven for about 1 hr.

Rye and Oatmeal Flour Bread

Dissolve 1 yeast cake in ¼ cup lukewarm water and ⅓ cup honey.

Boil 1⅓ cups water, 2 tsp. salt and 2 tbsp. oil.

Let cool to lukewarm, then mix with yeast mixture.

Mix 2 cups rye flour and ½ cup oatmeal flour.

Combine with the liquid mixture.

Add some more lukewarm water if necessary and make a firm dough.

Set the bowl in a warm place and let rise for about 2 hr.

Beat down with a wooden spoon for 2 or 3 min.

Put in a greased bread pan and let rise again for about 45 min.

Bake at 350°F about 50 to 60 min.

Buckwheat Bread

To 1 cup sugar add 2 cups buttermilk, 1 cup raisins and 2 tsp. salt.

Mix 1 tsp. baking powder with 4½ cups pure buckwheat flour.

Pour liquid into flour mixture and pour into 2 greased bread pans.

Bake in oven for 50 min.

ery good.

Date Rye Bread

Try

Mix ¼ cup brown sugar and 1 cup milk.

Mix 2½ cups rye flour, 1 tbsp. soy flour, 4 tsp. baking powder, 1 tsp. salt and 1 cup soaked, chopped dates.

Combine the mixtures and stir well.

Let stand 20 min in a greased pan, then bake 45 to 50 min.

Rye and Corn Bread

Dissolve 1 yeast cake in ¼ cup lukewarm water with 1 tbsp. honey, stirring until foamy.

Boil 1 cup water with 2½ tsp. salt and 2 tbsp. butter or lard.

When it is lukewarm, combine it with the yeast mixture.

Then mix 2¾ cups rye flour and ¼ cup cornmeal and add to mixture.

Set the bowl in a dishpan of quite warm water and let rise 1 hr or more.

Beat down with a wooden spoon for 2 min.

Put dough in a greased, floured bread pan and set it to rise again in a warm place covered with a towel.

When it is light, put it in the oven.

Turn the heat on and let it rise to 375°F.

Then turn the oven down to 325°F and bake for 1 hr.

 Fruit Bread

3 lb. dried pears and 3 lb. dried prunes should be soaked for 1 day.

Dice soaked fruits and save the liquid.

Also dice ½ lb. nuts, ½ lb. citron and ½ lb. figs.

Add 3½ lb. raisins, ½ lb. currants, 1 tsp. anise, 2 tsp. ground cinnamon, 1 tsp. ground cloves and ½ tsp. ground black pepper.

Make a soft dough from 3 lb. medium rye flour, 2 cakes of yeast and the liquid the fruit was soaked in.

Let rise until double.

Add all ingredients and allow to rise for another 45 min.

Place in greased bread pans and bake at 325°F for over 1 hr.

Keeps for months and tastes even better when allowed to age.

 Millet Bread with Carrots

Preheat oven to 375°F.

Pour ¾ cup boiling water over 1 cup millet flour and let cool.

Beat 3 egg whites stiff and set aside (save the yolks).

Mix ½ cup soy flour with 1 tsp. baking powder.

Add 3 egg yolks, 3 tbsp. oil, 1 tsp. sugar, a pinch of salt and 1 cup raw grated carrot.

Add soaked millet flour, fold egg whites into mixture and bake at once for 40 min.

Millet Sesame Bread ✓

Preheat oven to 450°F.

Combine 2 cups fine millet flour, ½ cup brown rice flour, ⅓ cup sesame meal, 1 tsp. salt and 2 tsp. baking powder.

Add 1 tbsp. oil, 1 tsp. honey and enough water to make a medium thick batter.

Pour batter into a bread pan or muffin tin, filling ⅔ full, and bake for 15 to 20 min.

If not well browned, put under the broiler for 1 min.

WHEAT FREE CAKES

Cheesecake

Press 24 oz cream cheese through a sieve.

Add 2 tbsp. lemon juice, 1½ cups sugar and 4 eggs.

Blend well and bake at 350°F for 35 min in a well greased cake pan.

Mix 16 oz sour cream with 2 tsp. cinnamon, ¾ cup sugar and 2 tbsp. lemon juice.

Pour this over cake and return to oven for 15 min.

Cake comes out soft but will harden when cooled.

Very excellent.

Oatmeal Cake with Carob

Pour 1½ cups boiling water over 1 cup uncooked rolled oats and let cool.

Cream ½ cup shortening with 2 eggs, 1¼ cup sugar and 1 tsp. vanilla.

Add oatmeal.

Stir in ½ cup carob powder or cocoa powder, 1½ cups rice flour and ½ cup oat flour which you sift with 2 tsp. baking powder.

Blend until smooth.

Pour in 8" x 12" greased pan and bake at 350°F for 35 to 40 min.

Potato Cake

Stir 6 egg yolks (save the whites) and 1 cup sugar until foamy, about 15 min.

Add 1 lb. potatoes which are boiled a day ahead and finely grated shortly before baking.

Add 2 tbsp. chopped almonds and 2 tsp. vanilla extract.

Fold in 6 egg whites whipped to a peak.

Bake immediately with moderate heat until done.

✿ Cottage Cheesecake

Cream ¼ lb. butter with 1 cup sugar.

Add 2 beaten eggs and 1 grated lemon peel.

Stir for 10 min.

Add 1 lb. cottage cheese and fold in 4 tbsp. corn meal, soy grit or millet grit mixed with 1 tsp. baking powder.

Pour into baking dish and bake for 1 hr at 300°F.

✿ Potato Biscuit Cake

Stir 4 egg yolks (save the whites) with 1 cup sugar until creamy and smooth.

Add a pinch of salt, ½ tsp. cinnamon, 1 tsp. lemon extract, 1 heaping tbsp. cocoa powder or carob powder and 28 almonds (slivered).

Grate ½ lb. boiled potatoes (boiled from the day before) on a fine grate and add to above mixture.

Mix thoroughly.

Beat 4 egg whites very stiff and add 2 tbsp. of either potato starch or cornstarch to it.

Fold into potato mixture, stirring little.

Fill in bread pan or cake pan and bake for 1 hr at 300°F.

Ⓧ ✿ Rice Flour Cake

Preheat oven to 325°F.

Stir until foamy ½ cup sugar, 4 egg yolks (save the whites), 1 tsp. almond extract and 2 tsp. vanilla.

Combine ½ cup rice flour with 1 tsp. baking powder and sift into batter.

Fold into dough 4 egg whites stiffly beaten.

Bake immediately for 45 min.

✿ Rye Bread Cake

Preheat oven to 325°F.

Stir until foamy 5 egg yolks (save the whites) and 1 cup sugar.

Add a dash of mace or cinnamon, 3 tbsp. chopped almonds and 5 tbsp. grated rye bread.

Add 5 egg whites stiffly beaten and fold into batter.

Bake for 30 min.

After cooling, frost with your favorite frosting.

Pound Cake

Cream ½ lb. butter and add ½ lb. sugar and 6 egg yolks (save the whites).

Continue stirring for ½ hr.

Add rum flavoring and ½ lb. potato flour, finest rice flour or cornstarch.

Fold into dough 6 egg whites stiffly beaten.

Bake for 1 hr at moderate heat.

Increase heat the last 15 min.

Keeps well in closed jar.

Carrot Torte

Beat 4 egg yolks (save the whites) with 2 tbsp. warm water and ¾ cup sugar for 5 min.

Add lemon or rum flavoring to it.

Beat 4 egg whites until stiff and add 1 tbsp. sugar.

Beat again until stiff and add to the egg yolks.

Combine 1 tsp. baking powder with 2 tbsp. potato starch, rice starch or cornstarch.

Add 1 cup ground almonds and 1 cup raw, finely grated carrots.

Mix everything and fill in your favorite cake pan.

Bake for 40 min in moderate oven.

Excellent.

Chestnut Cake

Bake 2 lb. chestnuts at 300°F for 20 min.

Peel and grate after they have cooled.

Cream 6 egg yolks (save the whites) with ½ cup sugar until foamy.

Add 2 tsp. vanilla extract and the grated chestnuts.

Fold in 6 egg whites stiffly beaten and bake immediately for 1 hr in moderate oven.

After cake is thoroughly cooled, cut in half and fill with a good jam.

Top with whipped cream or your favorite icing.

Almond Cake

Stir ¾ cup sugar with 2 eggs and 4 egg yolks (save the whites) for ½ hr or in a mixer for 8 min.

Add 1 cup ground almonds.

Mix and fold in 4 egg whites stiffly beaten.

Bake in a cake pan for 30 min at 300°F.

As soon as you take the cake out of the oven, pour ½ cup sweetened fruit juice over it and let it stand for several hours (raspberry juice is the finest).

Cherry Cake

Roast 4 slices rye bread in an oven and crumble thereafter.

Cream 5 egg yolks (save the whites) with 1 cup sugar until foamy and add ½ cup chopped nuts, the bread crumbs and 2 lb. pitted cherries (about 3 cups).

Fold in 5 egg whites stiffly beaten and bake for 1 hr at 350°F.

Oat Flour Cake

Mix 1 pt. of any sweetened fruit juice, ½ cup oil and 2 egg yolks (save the whites).

Beat very thoroughly (best results from blender).

Add 1 lb. Scotch style oatmeal or use rolled oats finely ground, ¼ lb. raisins, ¼ lb. dried prunes, ½ cup chopped almonds, 1 tsp. cinnamon and 2 tsp. baking powder.

Mix well.

Fold in 2 egg whites stiffly beaten.

Bake for 1 hr at 325°F.

Sweet Potato Cake

Mash 1 cup cooked sweet potatoes with 2 ripe bananas.

Add 1 cup milk and blend.

Add 2 tbsp. sugar, a dash of salt, 2 egg yolks and 3 tbsp. raisins.

Mix well and pour into a well greased baking dish.

Bake at 300°F for 45 min or until golden brown.

Millet Apple Cake

Cream very thoroughly ⅓ cup soy butter (milk free), ¾ cup raw or brown sugar, 2 eggs and 1 tsp. vanilla.

Mix 1½ cup fine millet flour with ¼ cup rice flour, 3 tsp. baking powder, ½ tsp. salt, ½ cup chopped nuts, ½ cup raisins, ½ tsp. nutmeg and ½ tsp. cinnamon.

If desired, ½ tsp. instant coffee may be added.

Combine moist and dry ingredients and gradually add 1 cup apple juice until smooth.

Pour into a 9" cake pan and bake at 375°F for 25 to 30 min or until done.

Millet Soufflé

Mix 1 cup millet grits with 3 cups hot water and 1 tsp. salt.

Cook over medium heat, stirring constantly until thick.

Beat 4 eggs, ½ cup whipping cream and 1 cup water until fluffy.

To this mixture add the hot grits, a small amount at a time.

Stir well and pour into oiled casserole.

Dot with butter or soy butter and bake at 300°F until set and slightly browned.

Johnny Cake

Mix together 2 cups cornmeal, 1½ tsp. salt, 1 tsp. baking powder and
2 tbsp. sugar.

Add 2 cups sour milk, yogurt or milk substitute (pg. 1), 2 beaten eggs and
2 tbsp. melted vegetable fat.

— substitute

Stir and pour into greased pan.

Bake at 400°F for 35 min.

Christmas Fruitcake

1 cup fine millet flour

¼ cup fine rye flour

¼ cup fine brown rice flour

2 tsp. baking powder

½ tsp. vegetable salt

½ cup honey

¼ cup apple juice

¾ cup grape juice

2 tsp. cinnamon

¼ tsp. allspice

¼ tsp. nutmeg

1 tbsp. grated lemon rind

1 tbsp. grated orange rind

1 cup chopped dates

1 cup seedless raisins

1 cup currants

1 cup pecans

1 cup sliced almonds

½ cup candied cherries

½ cup candied pineapple

(Continued on page 12)

1 tbsp. vanilla or rum flavoring

½ cup melted butter or soy butter

Prepare candied fruit a day ahead:

Drain the juice from water packed cherries and pineapples.

Boil honey until almost candied, add fruit and cook for 10 min.

Drain onto wax paper and store in tightly closed jars until ready for use.

Mix flours, spices, salt and baking powder.

Add chopped fruit and nuts.

Mix butter, juices and flavoring and add to flour mixture.

Mix in candied fruit.

Beat until evenly mixed.

Pour into well oiled and wax paper lined stem cake pan.

Bake at 300°F for 1 hr.

This cake will keep for months if wrapped in a grape juice soaked cheesecloth and tightly tinned.

WHEAT FREE COOKIES

  Honey Queen

Cream ½ cup butter with 3 tbsp. sugar.

Add 1 cup honey and 3 well beaten eggs or egg substitute (pg. 1).

Sift together 4 cups rye flour, 2 tsp. soda and 1 tsp. salt.

Add 2 cups flour mixture to honey mixture.

Beat hard for 2 min.

Stir in rest of flour and ½ cup nuts if desired.

Drop onto a greased cookie sheet 1½" apart.

Flatten lightly and bake at 325°F until done.

Very good.

Sugar Cookies

Preheat oven to 375°F.

Mix 1½ cups sifted powdered sugar and 1 cup butter.

Substitute Add 1 egg, 1 tsp. vanilla and ½ tsp. almond extract.

Blend 2½ cups rice flour with 1 tsp. soda and 1 tsp. cream of tartar.

Blend dry ingredients into moist ingredients and form a roll which you refrigerate for 2 to 3 hr.

With a knife, cut off small round pieces and bake until done.

✿ Carob Cookies

Beat 2 egg whites until stiff (you can save the yolks for the following recipe).

Add 1 cup instant carob powder, ½ cup sugar and ¾ cup chopped nuts.

Spoon small dots onto a greased cookie sheet and bake for 10 to 15 min at 350°F.

Let cookies cool on sheet, remove, turn over and let dry upside-down.

✿ Lemon Hearts   *Good*

Mix 3 egg yolks with ½ cup sugar and 1 tsp. lemon extract.

Add ½ lb. ground hazelnuts or almonds.   *plus enough white rice to make dough*

Roll dough on powdered sugar and shape into hearts or other designs.

Bake for 15 min at 350 to 400°F.   *325° For 12 mins.*

Frost the cookies with ½ cup powdered sugar and 1 tbsp. lemon juice while they are still hot.   *Drops on Pan*

Excellent.

✿ Buckwheat Cookies

Cream thoroughly 1 tbsp. butter and ½ cup brown sugar.

Add 2 tbsp. carob powder and 1 beaten egg.

Beat until fluffy.

Mix ½ tsp. soda with ⅔ cup sour cream.

Add 1 cup buckwheat flour and flavor with 1 tsp. vanilla extract.

Drop onto a greased cookie sheet and bake for 15 min at 350°F.

✿ Oatmeal Crisps

Cream ⅔ cup butter and 2 cups brown sugar until light and creamy.

Mix in 1 tsp. baking powder, ⅛ tsp. salt, 1 tsp. vanilla, 1 beaten egg, 2 tbsp. barley or soy flour and 2½ cups rolled oats.

Drop by teaspoonfuls 2" apart onto a greased cookie sheet.

Bake about 10 min at 350°F or until light brown.

Let cool a little before removing from the pan.

✿ Swedish Oatmeal Cookies

These cookies are worked by finger knead.

Make a solid mass of ⅔ cup butter, 3 cups rolled oats, ½ cup sugar, 1 beaten egg and 1 tsp. almond extract.

Form firmly into tiny balls and place onto a buttered cookie sheet.

Flatten with fork and bake at 325°F for 15 min or until nutty brown.

These cookies taste better when the dough has time to rest for ½ hr before forming into balls.

✿ Rye Cookies

Use above recipe but substitute rolled oats with cream of rye.

✿ Oatmeal Cookies

Brown in a frying pan 2 cups rolled oats with ½ cup butter until golden brown. Let cool.

Cream ½ cup butter with 1 cup sugar.

Add 2 beaten eggs, ½ cup nuts (optional) and 1 lemon rind.

Add to the toasted oats.

Drop by small spoonfuls onto a greased cookie sheet and bake at 350°F until light brown.

Very good.

✿ Oat Fruit Cookies

Blend thoroughly with blender or egg beater 1 cup cold water and 3 tbsp. oil.

Cut up or grind ½ lb. dried fruit and ½ cup nuts.

Add 1 cup ground rolled oats or Scotch style oatmeal and 1 tsp. baking powder.

Add the water-oil mixture and knead thoroughly.

Add more oats if needed to roll out.

Cut squares and bake until done in moderate oven.

✿ Coconut Balls

Boil 2 cups sugar with 1 cup water to "soft ball" stage.

Add 1 tsp. vanilla.

Pour mixture over 2 egg whites stiffly beaten and beat until light and fluffy.

Stir in 2 cups shredded coconut.

Drop onto a buttered cookie sheet by teaspoonfuls.

Bake at 300°F for 20 min.

Coconut Macaroons

Beat 4 egg whites until stiff.

Add a pinch of cinnamon.

Mix 1 cup grated coconut with ½ cup sugar and fold into egg whites.

Drop onto a greased cookie sheet and bake 30 min at moderate heat.

Rye Squares

Preheat oven to 350°F.

Mix ½ cup rye flour, ½ cup rolled oats, 1 cup nuts, ½ tsp. salt and ½ tsp. baking powder.

In a mixing bowl combine 2 eggs or Egg Substitute #2 (pg. 1), 1 cup sugar, ⅓ cup oil and ½ tsp. vanilla.

Beat until creamy and smooth.

Add slowly to dry ingredients and stir well.

Pour into well greased 9" pan and bake for 35 min.

Let cool and cut into squares.

Very good.

Applesauce Cookies

Mix 1 cup raisins with 1 cup applesauce and set aside for ½ hr.

Cream ½ cup butter with 1 cup sugar and 1 egg or egg substitute (pg. 1).

Add a pinch each of cinnamon, nutmeg, cloves and salt.

Mix 1 cup rice flour with ½ cup soy flour.

Add 1 tsp. baking powder.

Blend all ingredients and work in 1 cup Rice Krispies™ or puffed millet.

Make little dots on cookie sheet, flatten lightly and bake at 325°F for 25 min.

Coconut Cookies

Beat thoroughly 3 eggs, ½ cup honey and 2 tbsp. oil.

Add 2 cups coconut shreds.

Pour mixture into 1½ cups oat flour in which you blend 1 tsp. baking powder.

Mix thoroughly and drop small cookies onto cookie sheet.

Flatten lightly and decorate with ½ candied cherry or piece of candied orange peel.

Bake at 325°F for 20 min.

Oat Cookies

Cream ¼ lb. butter, ¾ cup sugar and 2 eggs until fluffy.

Add 1 tsp. lemon or vanilla flavoring.

Fold in 1 lb. finely ground Scotch style oatmeal or rolled oats and enough milk or soya milk (pg. 2) that dough can be spooned out.

Spoon cookies onto a well greased cookie sheet and place a bit of your favorite jam in the middle of each cookie.

Bake at 350°F until golden brown.

French Cookies

Beat 4 egg whites until stiff.

Gradually add ¾ cup sugar.

Place on greased cookie sheet in small, pretty heaps.

You may decorate them with a tiny piece of cherry in the center.

The oven should be almost cold when you start baking and very little heat should be applied.

The cookies should turn just a little yellow.

X

Almond Macaroons

Beat 2 egg whites until stiff.

Add ½ cup sugar, ½ cup ground or finely chopped almonds and a pinch of cinnamon.

Drop little cookies onto a greased baking sheet and bake for 30 min at moderate heat.

Almond Cookies

Beat 2 egg whites until they hold a peak.

Add 1 cup sugar and 1 tsp. vanilla.

Blend in 1 cup ground almonds.

Drop by teaspoonfuls onto a greased baking sheet and bake for 35 min at 275°F.

Sunflower Seed Cookies

Follow above recipe but use ground sunflower seeds instead of ground almonds.

X

Easy Rice Cookies

Combine 1 cup sugar with 2 large eggs in a saucepan.

Bring to a boil stirring constantly for 1 to 2 min.

almonds

Remove from heat and stir in 3 cups Rice Krispies™ and ½ cup chopped nuts or coconut (optional).

or walnuts

Shape cooled dough into small balls and roll in ground nuts or coconuts.
Store in a closed jar.

Surprisingly good.

Raisin Cookies

Simmer ½ cup raisins in 1 cup water and let cool.

Cream 1½ cups brown sugar with ½ cup butter or shortening.

Add 2 beaten eggs or egg substitute (pg. 1) and raisin mixture.

Sift 2 cups rye flour, 2 tsp. salt, 1 tsp. soda, 1 tsp. cinnamon, 1 cup oatmeal, 1 tsp. vanilla and nuts (optional).

Add to mixture. (dough should be quite thin.).

Drop by spoonfuls onto a greased cookie sheet.

Bake at 350°F for 10 to 15 min.

Peanut Butter Cookies

Mix ¾ cup peanut butter, ¾ cup sugar and 2 tbsp. tapioca or rice flour.

Add 1 egg white beaten until slightly stiff.

Form a roll and refrigerate for 1 to 2 hr.

Cut roll into slices and bake on greased cookie sheet at 350°F until done.

WHEAT FREE MUFFINS

Rice Flour and Millet Biscuits

Sift ½ cup millet flour, ⅓ cup rice flour, 1 tsp. baking powder and ¾ tsp. salt.

Add 1 tbsp. oil, 1 tbsp. butter and ½ cup milk to make a very soft dough.

Form dough into 11 or 12 biscuits with hands.

Bake on a greased, floured tin in a very hot oven about 25 min.

Rye and Rice Flour Muffins

Mix and sift 1 cup rye flour, ½ cup whole rice flour, 1½ tsp. baking powder, 1 tsp. salt and 2 tbsp. brown sugar.

Add ¼ cup dried currants.

Mix ½ cup sour cream, 1 beaten egg and ½ cup buttermilk.

Combine the liquid with the dry ingredients and stir in about ¼ cup more buttermilk, enough to make a fluffy dough, stirring as little as possible.

Bake in 9 greased and floured muffin tins at 375°F for 15 min, then at 300°F for 5 min longer.

These are filling and delicious muffins for anyone, especially those on a wheat free diet.

Soy Muffins

Sift and mix 1½ cups soy flour, 2 tsp. baking powder and 1 tsp. salt.

Cream very thoroughly 2 egg yolks (save the whites) with 3 tbsp. brown or raw sugar and 1 tbsp. melted butter.

Slowly add 1 cup milk and pour into dry ingredients. *Use soy milk*

Add ¼ cup raisins and ¼ cup chopped nuts. *(½ c. chopped almonds)*

Fold in 2 egg whites stiffly beaten.

Pour into greased muffin tins and bake at 375°F for 30 min.

This makes deliciously light, fluffy muffins.

WHEAT FREE PANCAKES

Fried Millet for Breakfast

Prepare a thick millet cereal.

When done, stir in 1 egg yolk and 1 tbsp. butter.

Pour onto a greased plate and let it become cold and thick.

Cut up into cakes and fry in butter until light brown on both sides.

Potato Pancakes

For each person cook 1 medium sized potato, peel and grate.

Add some salt.

Shape pancakes and bake in a frying pan in hot oil until golden brown on both sides.

You may add 1 egg or egg substitute (pg. 1), wheat free flour of your choice, onions and parsley.

Oat and Apple Pancakes

Mix 3 cups rolled oats with 2 cups milk or soya milk (pg. 2) and let stand for 1 hr.

Add 2 egg yolks, 2 egg whites stiffly beaten, 3 tbsp. ground almonds and a pinch of salt.

Fold into batter 2 lb. grated apples.

Bake pancakes in frying pan in hot oil or other good fat.

Serve with sugar and cinnamon.

Very delicious.

Barley and Soy Flour Pancakes

Sift 1 cup barley flour with ⅓ cup soy flour.

Mix in 1½ tsp. baking powder, 1 tsp. salt and 2 tsp. sugar.

Add 1 cup buttermilk or ½ cup sour cream and ½ cup milk.

Stir for 1 min.

Fry in oil on a hot pancake griddle.

Serve with butter and maple syrup.

 ## Oatmeal Pancakes

Sift and mix ⅞ cup oatmeal flour, ½ tsp. soda, 1 tsp. baking powder and 1 tsp. salt.

Mix 1 tbsp. honey or syrup, 3 tbsp. sour cream, 1 tbsp. melted butter and 1 beaten egg.

Combine, drop by spoonfuls onto a greased pan and bake on both sides until brown.

 ## Oat Pancakes

Soak 3 cups rolled oats in 1 pt. water for 3 hr.

Add 3 beaten eggs, 1 tbsp. sugar and ¾ cup of either oat flour, barley flour or tapioca flour.

Drop small pancakes onto frying pan with heated oil and fry until crisp on both sides.

 ## Buckwheat Flour Pancakes

Dissolve ⅓ yeast cake in ½ cup warm water.

Mix ¾ cup boiling water with 2 cups buckwheat flour.

When lukewarm, combine with the yeast and add 1 cup milk, 1 tsp. salt, 1 tbsp. molasses and 4 tbsp. melted butter.

Set in a warm place and let rise overnight.

Fry on a hot, well greased griddle and serve with maple syrup.

 ## Vegetable Pancakes

Soak 1 cup rolled oats in 1 cup milk or milk substitute (pg. 1) for ½ hr.

Add 2 beaten eggs and finely cut vegetables (cauliflower, asparagus, parsley, onions, mushrooms or any leftover vegetable).

Heat oil or other good fat in a frying pan and bake the pancakes very slowly.

Serve with tossed salad.

✸ Rye Pancakes

Mix ¾ cup rye flour, ½ tsp. baking powder, ½ tsp. soda, 1 tsp. salt and ⅓ cup brown sugar.

Beat 1 egg, 1 tbsp. melted butter and 1 cup buttermilk.

Combine the mixtures, thinning with a little more buttermilk if necessary, but do not stir very much.

Fry on a hot, greased griddle.

Serve with syrup.

✸ Millet Dish

Bring 3½ cups water or soya milk (pg. 2) to a boil.

Add 1 cup washed millet and a dash of salt and simmer for 35 to 45 min.

Add 2 tbsp. soy butter and cool.

Then spread mixture onto cookie sheet and sprinkle with sugar and cinnamon.

Bake for 20 min in a hot oven.

Very tasty with applesauce or stewed fruit.

✸ Barley Yeast Pancakes

Soak 1 tbsp. yeast in ½ cup lukewarm water.

Mix 2 cups barley flour, 1 egg, 2 tbsp. honey, 1 tsp. salt and 4 tbsp. oil.

Work in yeast and as much water as needed to make consistency of a heavy pancake mix.

Let stand for 10 min and bake on medium heated griddle.

Serve with some preserves.

Very good.

WHEAT FREE PIE CRUSTS

Ⓧ ✸ Rice Flour Pie Crust

Make rice flour cake dough (pg. 8).

Pour dough into 2 pie pans.

Bake until light brown and let cool.

Fill with your favorite pie filling and top with the other baked crust.

✸ Coconut Pie Crust

Spread 2 tbsp. soft vegetable shortening in a 9" pie pan.

Sprinkle with 1½ to 2 cups shredded coconut.

Pat evenly and bake at 350°F for 10 min.

✳ ❆ Rice Flakes Pie Crust

Mix 2 cups rice flour or rice flakes, ⅓ cup powdered sugar and ¼ tsp. cinnamon.

Pour ½ cup melted butter or milk free butter substitute over it and pat evenly in a 9" pie pan.

Bake for 10 min in a hot oven or place in refrigerator for several hours.

❆ Barley Flour Pie Crust

Mix ⅓ cup barley flour, ⅔ cup whole rice flour, 1 tsp. salt, ⅓ cup lard or butter, ice water and 2 tbsp. soft butter.

Prepare the pie crust as usual.

❆ Oat Flour Pie Crust

Cream ⅓ cup butter with 2 tbsp. honey or sugar.

Slowly add 1¼ cups oat flour (1 tbsp. water may be needed).

Press into a well greased pie pan and bake 15 min at 375°F.

Excellent for raw fruit filling.

❆ Shortcake Pie Crust

Stir together well 1 beaten egg or egg substitute (pg. 1), 2 tbsp. brown or raw sugar, 1 tbsp. melted butter, ½ tsp. salt and some mace or cinnamon.

Mix 2 cups soy flour, 3 tsp. baking powder and 1½ cups milk.

Combine mixtures.

Bake in pie pan at 350°F for 40 min.

Fill with your favorite fruit.

- *You may create a yeast free recipe by using unbleached whole grain flours, aluminum free baking powder, unrefined sugars (or sugar substitutes) and unrefined oils (cold pressed or expeller pressed).*
- *Cereal free baking powder is recommended where baking powder is indicated (pg. 2).*

EGG, MILK AND WHEAT FREE CAKES

✿ Carob Cake

Cream 2 cups brown sugar, ½ cup oil, ¾ cup soya milk or soya milk yogurt (pg. 2) and juice of ½ lemon.

Add 1 heaping tbsp. Egg Substitute #1 or #2 (pg. 1), 1 cup cold mashed potatoes and 8 tbsp. instant carob powder.

Sift 2 cups rice flour with 3 tsp. baking powder and 1 cup nuts (optional).

Fold ingredients together and add 1 cup puffed millet or puffed rice (this makes the product light).

Bake for 40 min at 350°F.

After cooling make a white icing.

Works fine for cupcakes, too.

✿ Sunday Cake   *Crisco*

Beat 1 cup brown sugar, ½ cup oil and 2 tbsp. egg substitute (pg. 1).

Add 4 tbsp. carob powder and 2 tsp. instant coffee (makes it elegant).

Mix 1 cup soy flour, 1 cup rice flour and 3 tsp. baking powder.

Combine ingredients and add about 1 cup soya milk (pg. 2) to make to cake consistency.

Bake at 350°F for 40 to 45 min.

White frosting furnishes a tasty and wholesome cake.

✿ Spice Cake

Boil 1 cup raisins, 1 cup sugar, 1/2 cup oil and 4 oz mixed candied fruit in 1½ cups water.

Let cool and add 1 cup rice flour, ½ cup soy flour and 1 cup cornmeal mixed with 4 tsp. baking powder.

Add 2 tsp. cinnamon and 1 tsp. instant coffee.

Bake in loaf pan at 350°F for almost 1 hr.

✳ White Cake

Mix 1½ cups sugar, 1½ cups cold, iced potatoes, ½ cup oil, 2 tsp. vanilla and ½ tsp. salt.

Mix 1 cup rice flour, 1 cup potato starch and 4 tsp. baking powder.

Combine ingredients and add ⅓ to ½ cup cold water (until dough begins to get smooth).

Bake at 375°F for ½ hr.

✳ Banana Cake

Sift 1½ cups brown rice flour with 2 tsp. baking powder.

Add a pinch each of salt, cinnamon, nutmeg and cloves.

Mash 2 ripe bananas and blend with 5 tbsp. oil, ¾ cup sugar and 2 tbsp. egg substitute (pg. 1).

Add water if needed and blend all ingredients.

Pour into a well greased pan and bake at 375°F.

EGG, MILK AND WHEAT FREE COOKIES

✳ Almond and Rice Flour Cookies

Cream ½ cup soy butter and 4 tbsp. sugar until smooth.

Add ¾ cup browned ground almonds and 2 tsp. almond extract.

Add 1½ cups rice flour and mix.

Roll little spoonfuls between the palms of the hands and lay on baking sheet.

Bake at 375°F for 8 min.

They may be rolled in powdered sugar if desired and become firm when they cool.

Makes 46.

✳ Honey Cookies N^o

Heat 11/2 lb. honey to a boiling point.

Add 1/2 lb. chopped almonds and take from heat.

Add 4 oz chopped citron, 4 oz orange, 1 tsp. cinnamon and a dash each of cardamom and cloves.

Let cool.

Add to 2 lb. Scotch style oatmeal or rolled oats.

Add 2 tsp. baking powder and knead thoroughly.

The dough has to rest for 24 hr.

Next day roll it out and cover 2 or 3 cookie sheets with it.

Bake in moderate oven and then cut into squares or diagonal pieces.

You may frost them with a very thin frosting if you like.

These cookies soften with age, are very tasty and keep well in a closed jar.

❀ Pumpkin Cookies

Mix thoroughly ½ cup honey and ½ cup oil.

Add 1½ cup mashed pumpkin, 1 tsp. lemon extract and 1 tsp. vanilla.

Mix 2½ cups rice flour, 2 cups quinoa flour, 1cup tapioca flour, 2 tsp. baking powder and ¼ tsp. salt.

Blend everything to "drop cookie" consistency.

Place onto a greased cookie sheet, flatten with fork and bake at 350°F for 20 min.

❀ Hazelnut Cookies

Cream or mix in blender ½ stick milk free butter or ¼ cup oil, ½ cup sugar, 1 tsp. vanilla, 4 tbsp. water and 1 tbsp. Egg Substitute #2 (pg. 1).

Add 1 cup ground hazelnuts.

Work in ¾ cup rice flour in which you mix 1 tsp. baking powder.

Form small cookies and bake at 325°F until brown.

 ## ❀ Soya Cookies

Cream thoroughly ½ cup oil, ½ cup warmed honey and ¾ cup brown sugar.

Add 1 grated lemon rind, the juice of 1 lemon and 2 tbsp. egg substitute (pg. 1). *or 2 eggs*

Mix 1½ cups soy flour, 1½ cups low fat soy powder and 3 tsp. baking powder.

Knead, roll out dough and form cookies with cutter.

Moisten the tops with an Egg Substitute (pg. 1) and sprinkle heavily with chopped nuts and coarse sugar.

Bake at 325°F for 20 to 25 min.

❀ Lemon Cookies

Mix thoroughly ½ cup honey, ½ cup oil or 1 stick milk free butter, 2 tbsp. Egg Substitute #1 (pg. 1) and 3 finely grated lemon rinds.

Add 1¼ cups rice flour mixed with 1 tsp. baking powder.

Bake a sample of drop cookies.

If too soft add 1 tbsp. rice flour (lower altitudes need more flour).

Bake for 20 min at 350°F.

 ## ❀ Gingersnaps

Mix ½ cup blackstrap molasses, 3 tbsp. oil, 3 rounded tbsp. brown sugar and ½ cup soya milk (pg. 2) or water.

Add ½ tsp. ginger, 1 tsp. cinnamon, 1 tsp. allspice and 1 tbsp. Egg Substitute #2 (pg. 1). *1 egg*

Pour everything into a mixture of 1 cup rice flour, 1 cup soy flour or oat flour and 2 tsp. baking powder.

Stir and spoon onto a greased cookie sheet.

Bake at 400°F for 15 min.

✺ Flax Seed Cookies

Mix in blender or beat for 3 to 4 min 1½ cups sugar, ½ cup oil and 4 tbsp. water.

Add 2 tsp. cinnamon and 1 cup Egg Substitute #2 (pg. 1).

Sift 2 cups rice flour with 2 tsp. baking powder.

Fold blended mixture into flour mixture.

Spread onto a greased cookie sheet and bake at 325°F until light brown.

Cut into small strips and loosen from sheet.

Put back in oven (heat turned off) and crisp for a few min.

Take out and roll in coarse sugar.

You may add ½ cup pecans for a change.

Very good.

✺ Peanut Butter Goodies #1

Cream ½ cup peanut butter and ½ cup sugar.

Add 1½ cups puffed millet.

Form round balls.

Bake on a greased cookie sheet at 350°F until brown.

Let cool on sheet.

✺ Peanut Butter Goodies #2

Cream peanut butter and sugar as above.

Add 1¼ cups puffed rice (rice has to be crushed with a rolling pin).

Bake as above.

Does not have to cool on sheet.

✺ Peanut Butter Goodies #3

Cream peanut butter and sugar as above.

Add 2 heaping tbsp. Egg Substitute #2 (pg. 1).

Form small cookies and bake at 325°F for 15 min.

EGG, MILK AND WHEAT FREE MAYONNAISE

Delicious and wholesome mayonnaise can be made without egg or milk.

🌟 Egg, Milk and Wheat Free Mayonnaise #1

Mix in blender 1 cup safflower, soy or sunflower oil, a dash of salt and 1 tbsp. lemon juice.

Add 1 cup water and ½ avocado (or more if you like it thick).

For variety add parsley, tomato or tarragon.

🌟 Egg, Milk and Wheat Free Mayonnaise #2

Mix in blender 1 cup safflower, soy or sunflower oil with 1 cup water, 1 large tomato, a dash of salt and 1 tsp. honey.

🌟 Egg, Milk and Wheat Free Mayonnaise #3

Mix in blender ½ cup safflower, soy or sunflower oil, 1½ cups water and ¾ cup nuts.

Sweeten with sugar or honey and serve on fruit salads.

✳ 🌟 Egg, Milk and Wheat Free Mayonnaise #4

Mix in blender until thick 1 cup tahini (liquefied sesame seed) and 2 tbsp. honey.

Serve on fruit salads or use as a sandwich spread.

Very nourishing.

🌟 Egg, Milk and Wheat Free Mayonnaise #5

Soya milk mayonnaise: Blend until well mixed 3 tbsp. soya milk powder (or 4 tbsp. instant) and 1/2 cup water for a few seconds.

Add 1/2 cup safflower, soy or sunflower oil, pouring in a steady, small stream.

Add 1 tsp. honey or raw sugar and salt, garlic salt, onion salt and paprika to taste.

Blend well.

Add 1/2 cup more oil and continue blending until thick.

Slowly add 1/4 cup lemon juice.

Blend for a few seconds after all the juice has been added.

Place in covered container and refrigerate.

EGG, MILK AND WHEAT FREE PIE CRUSTS

🌟 Barley Flour Pie Crust

Whip 4 tbsp. oil, 3½ tbsp. water and 1 tsp. salt.

Add 1½ cups barley flour and 1 tsp. baking powder.

Work into a 9" pie crust.

Other Pie Crust Suggestions

■ Crushed rice flakes, milk free butter or oil and sugar.

■ Crushed corn flakes, milk free butter or oil and sugar.

■ Crushed matzo, sugar, oil and water.

■ Grated nuts, sugar, milk free butter or oil and water.

■ Crushed rye crisp, sugar, milk free butter or oil and water.

■ Ground sunflower seeds, water and sugar.

YEAST FREE DIET

■ *For yeast free recipes be sure to use unbleached whole grain flours, aluminum free baking powder, unrefined sugars (or sugar substitutes) and unrefined oils (cold pressed or expeller pressed).*

■ *Egg substitutes may be used where eggs are indicated (pg. 1).*

■ *Milk substitutes may be used where milk is indicated (pg. 1).*

■ *Cereal free baking powder is recommended where baking powder is indicated (pg. 2).*

YEAST FREE BREADS

Bread

½ cup oat flour

½ cup potato flour

½ cup barley flour

2 tbsp. honey

½ tsp. salt

4 tsp. aluminum free baking powder

2 tbsp. unrefined oil

¾ cup water

1 egg (optional)

Preheat oven to 375°F.

Combine dry ingredients.

In a separate dish, beat with egg beater or by hand all the wet ingredients. (The longer you beat the better the bread will be!)

Quickly fold dry and moist ingredients together and bake for 30 to 35 min until done.

Makes 2 loaves.

Steamed Corn Bread (Unleavened)

Dissolve 1 tsp. aluminum free baking powder in 2¾ cups milk.

Add ½ tsp. salt and 2 tbsp. unrefined sugar.

Mix 4 cups coarse white cornmeal and ¾ cup rice flour.

Add to mixture.

Stir in 1 tbsp. melted butter and 1 egg stiffly beaten.

Steam 2 hr or more, then brown in oven.

 Southern Spoon Bread (Unleavened)

Add 1 cup coarse white cornmeal to 2 cups milk and bring to a boiling point, constantly stirring, until it is a smooth mush.

Remove from heat, cool and add 1 tsp. salt, 3 beaten egg yolks (save the whites) and 2 tbsp. butter.

Mix thoroughly and fold in 3 egg whites stiffly beaten.

Bake in oven.

Serve in baking dish.

 Rolls

Mix thoroughly with a blender or an egg beater 2 cups cold water, 2 cups cold milk or soya milk (pg. 2), 2 tbsp. unrefined oil, 2 tsp. unrefined sugar and 1 tsp. salt.

To 3 cups yeast free flour (unbleached) add 2 tsp. aluminum free baking powder.

Pour liquid ingredients into flour and make a firm dough.

If needed, add more flour.

Knead well (70 strokes) and form rolls.

Cut tops with scissors and sprinkle with poppy seeds or caraway seeds.

Bake at 375°F for ½ hr.

 Prune Bread

Mix ½ cup rice flour or soy flour, 1 cup cornmeal, 4 tsp. aluminum free baking powder, 1 tsp. salt and 1 cup soaked, pitted and sliced prunes.

Mix 1 tbsp. melted shortening or a butter and unrefined oil mixture, 1 cup milk and ¼ cup molasses.

Combine with flour mixture.

Let stand in a greased bread pan 25 min.

Bake slowly for 1 hr.

Matzo

Beat very thoroughly in blender or by hand 1 cup cold water and 2 tbsp. unrefined oil.

Add enough yeast free flour that dough can be rolled out easily.

Roll dough very thin, cut into desired shapes, prick with a fork and bake in a hot oven until light brown.

✵ Diet Bread from Oats

Beat thoroughly 2 cups water and 2 tbsp. unrefined oil.

Add ½ lb. rolled oats and so much oat flour until you cannot handle it.

Work in 2 tsp. aluminum free baking powder and some salt if desired.

Form flat, round cakes and bake in moderate oven for ½ hr or until done.

✵ Bread from Arabia

Beat thoroughly in blender or by hand 3 cups cold water, 2 tbsp. unrefined oil, 1 tsp. salt and 2 tsp. unrefined sugar.

After mixture is well emulsified add so much yeast free flour that dough can be rolled out.

Cut flat, round cakes and bake them on a greased cookie sheet at 400°F for 20 min.

✵ Rice Barley Bread

Preheat oven to 375°F.

Sift: 1 cup barley flour

           1 cup rice flour

           2 tbsp. aluminum free baking powder

           For a variation, add ½ cup rye flour

Add: 2 tbsp. unrefined oil

           ½ tsp. salt

           2 tbsp. honey

           4 oz water

Beat well by hand or beater.

Depending on dryness of flour, more water should be added until dough is smooth.

Bake for 30 min (in high altitudes bake longer).

❄ Thanksgiving Bread

Mix: 1 cup rice flour

          1 cup oat flour (ground rolled oats)

          1 cup potato starch flour or cornstarch

          6 tsp. aluminum free baking powder

Boil: 1 cup cranberries

          1 cup unrefined sugar

          1 cup water

Add: 3 tbsp. butter

Let cool.

Grate 1 orange peel for flavor and also squeeze the juice of this 1 orange.

Stir this and 1 egg into cranberry mixture.

Mix dry and moist ingredients together.

Add ½ cup or more nuts.

Bake in 2 small loaves for 45 to 55 min at 375°F.

❄ Gingerbread

Mix: 1 cup rice flour

          1 cup barley flour

          5 tsp. aluminum free baking powder

Set aside.

Preheat oven to 350°F.

Take a saucepan and mix the following ingredients:

      ½ cup water

      ½ cup blackstrap molasses

      ½ cup honey

      ½ cup unrefined oil

      ½ tsp. ginger

      ½ tsp. salt

      1 tsp. cinnamon

      1 tsp. ground nutmeg

Place over low heat and let dissolve well, stirring constantly.

Let mixture cool.

Add 2 eggs (optional).

Combine all ingredients and spread thickly onto a cookie sheet.

Bake for 20 min or until done.

Cut into pieces after it is somewhat cooled.

Carrot Almond Torte

1 tbsp. butter
¼ cup crushed almond macaroons
3 medium carrots, peeled and grated
1½ cups toasted, blanched almonds
4 eggs, separated
1 cup unrefined sugar
1 tsp. vanilla extract
1 tbsp. grated orange rind
¼ cup cornstarch or arrowroot starch
1 tsp. aluminum free baking powder

Preheat oven to 350°F.

Grease a 9" springform pan with butter.

Sprinkle the bottom and sides with crushed almond macaroons.
Set aside.

Place carrots in a large mixing bowl.

Grate almonds in blender until chopped very fine and add to carrots.

In another bowl beat egg yolks, sugar and vanilla with an electric mixer until thick and lemon colored.

Add this and grated orange rind to carrot-almond mixture.

Sift starch and baking powder together and add to mixture.

Stir until thoroughly combined.

Fold in stiffly beaten egg whites.

Pour batter into prepared pan.

Bake for 35 to 40 min.

Cool to room temperature and remove springform.

✨ Tasty Orange Cake

Take 2 oranges and, with a fine grater, take the orange rind off the white part.

Squeeze oranges so you have 1 cup juice.

Place rind and juice in a bowl and add ½ cup honey , 2 eggs, 3 tbsp. unrefined oil, ½ cup unrefined sugar and a dash of salt.

Beat well.

Sift together 1 cup barley flour, 1 cup rice flour and 4 tsp. aluminum free baking powder.

Add moist ingredients to dry ingredients and bake slowly at 350°F for 1 hr or until done.

Flour mixture can also be rye and rice flour or barley and millet flour. In any case it is good!

✨ Corn Spice Cake

Simmer in 1¼ cups water for 15 min the following ingredients:

> 1 cup raisins
>
> 2 oz chopped citron
>
> ½ cup unrefined oil
>
> 1 cup unrefined sugar
>
> 1 tsp. cinnamon
>
> ½ tsp. salt

Cool and pour into a mixture of:

> 1 cup fine cornmeal
>
> 1 cup rye flour
>
> 4 tsp. aluminum free baking powder

Mix well and bake for 45 min at 375°F.

Cake pan has to be well greased and sprinkled with cornmeal.

✨ Potato Sponge Cake

Preheat oven to 350°F.

Beat 4 egg yolks (save the whites), continue beating and slowly pour in ¾ cup honey.

Add 1 tbsp. lemon juice and ½ lemon rind finely grated.

Fold in ½ cup sifted potato starch.

Beat the 4 egg whites stiff to a peak, fold them in and bake in a pan which is only greased at the bottom, not on the sides, so cake can "climb."

Bake for 35 min.

After cooling, loosen with a knife.

✸ Rice Flour Chocolate or Yellow Cupcakes   *Make*

¾ cup rice flour

1 tsp. soda

½ tsp. salt

⅔ cup unrefined sugar

2 tbsp. cocoa (omit if yellow cakes are desired)

½ cup butter

1 egg unbeaten

⅝ cup milk (½ cup + ⅛ cup; ⅛ cup = 2 tbsp.) (add 1 tsp. vinegar to milk)

½ tsp. vanilla

Sift rice flour, soda, cocoa and salt 3 times.

In a large bowl beat butter and sugar together, then add egg and beat until light and fluffy.

Combine milk and vanilla and add to liquid mixture.

Alternately beat in flour mixture and liquid mixture until smooth.

Let stand about 5 to 10 min to allow rice flour to absorb moisture.

Place paper baking cups into muffin tins and fill each one about ¾ full.

Bake in preheated oven at 350°F for 20 to 25 min or until a toothpick comes out clean.

Ice with favorite icing.

Makes 1 dozen cupcakes.

YEAST FREE COOKIES

✸ Carrot Cookies

Mix: 1 cup rice flour

2 tbsp. soy flour or barley flour

2 tsp. aluminum free baking powder

1 cup raisins (these should be covered with flour and set aside)

Cream: ½ cup butter (1 stick) or unrefined oil

½ cup honey

2 tbsp. unrefined sugar

3 eggs (optional if soy flour is used)

Add: 2 tsp. cinnamon

A dash of cloves

½ tsp. ginger

2 cups finely shredded carrots (the finer the carrots the better the cookies!).

(Continued on page 34)

Mix dry and moist ingredients and add water if needed so you can make drop cookies (some carrots have more fluid than others).

Bake on an oiled cookie sheet for 20 min at 350°F.

Rice Flour Wafers

> ¼ cup butter
>
> ¼ cup unrefined sugar
>
> 1 egg
>
> 1 grated lemon rind
>
> ¾ cup sifted rice flour

Cream butter and sugar.

Add egg and grated lemon rind.

Stir in flour, blending well.

Sprinkle rice flour on board and roll dough thin.

Bake in 400°F oven until golden brown, about 8 min.

Simple, easy and good.

YEAST FREE CRACKERS

Crackers

To 1 cup cold water add 3 tbsp. oil, 1 tsp. salt and 2 tsp. unrefined sugar.

Beat thoroughly in blender or by hand until well emulsified.

Pour into 2 cups of yeast free flour mix and add more flour if needed until dough can be rolled.

Roll as thin as you like your cracker.

Sprinkle with coarse salt and caraway seeds and bake in moderate oven until well done.

Oatmeal Cakes

Mix thoroughly 1 cup rye flour, 2 cups steel cut oatmeal, ½ tsp. salt and 2 or 3 tbsp. butter.

Add ½ to ¾ cup cold water to make a stiff dough.

Knead well and roll into very thin cakes.

Bake in a moderately hot oven until brown.

✴ Cheese Stars

> ½ cup grated cheese
>
> ½ cup grated sunflower seeds or nuts
>
> 1 tbsp. unrefined oil or butter
>
> 1 cup rye flour
>
> 2 tsp. aluminum free baking powder

Mix by hand and add water if needed.

Roll out like you would do cookies and with a cutter make stars, wedges or squares.

Bake for 15 min in moderate oven.

YEAST FREE MUFFINS

✴ Pineapple Muffins   *Tastes Good*

Preheat oven to 375°F.   *350°*

Sift into a bowl:

> 2 cups rice flour
>
> 3 tsp. aluminum free baking powder
>
> ½ tsp. salt
>
> ½ tsp. nutmeg

Cream:

> 1 egg
>
> 4 tbsp. unrefined oil or butter
>
> ½ cup unrefined sugar or honey

Drizzle on after Baking.

Add:

> 1 cup crushed pineapple (save the juice)

use the juice

Fold into dry ingredients and add pineapple juice if needed for more moisture.

Bake in greased muffin tins for 20 min.

While muffins are still hot drip the butter-honey mixture on them.

ery tasty!

YEAST FREE NOODLES

> ⅓ cup rice flour
>
> 1 egg
>
> ½ tsp. aluminum free baking powder
>
> ¼ tsp. salt

Combine rice flour, baking powder and salt.

Add beaten egg and knead into a smooth dough.

When dough is too stiff, add sufficient moisture to make a soft dough to roll.

(Continued on page 36)

Dust board with rice flour, place dough on it and roll out to desired thickness.

Allow to dry for a short while, then cut into narrow strips.

Continue to dry until noodles can be easily picked up and handled.

Cook in boiling water or broth.

When not used immediately, noodles should be placed in a plastic bag in the refrigerator for storage.

YEAST FREE PIE CRUST

Try

¾ cup rice flour

1 tsp. unrefined sugar

½ tsp. salt

¼ cup shortening or oil-butter mixture

¼ to ½ cup warm water

Mix dry ingredients and work fat into them.

Add water to make soft dough.

Let stand about 10 min before rolling out to place on tin.

Bake at 350°F degrees for about 20 min.

GLUTEN FREE BREAD

- *Egg substitutes may be used where eggs are indicated (pg. 1).*
- *Milk substitutes may be used where milk is indicated (pg. 1).*
- *Cereal free baking powder is recommended where baking powder* ~~Good~~
  is indicated (pg. 2).
- *You may create a yeast free recipe by using unbleached whole grain flours,
  aluminum free baking powder, unrefined sugars (or sugar substitutes) and
  unrefined oils (cold pressed or expeller pressed).* make

    ¾ cup rice polishings or white rice flour

    ¼ cup potato starch flour

    ¼ cup pure bulk soy flour

    4 tsp. aluminum free baking powder

    1 tsp. salt

    2 tbsp. unrefined sugar

    3 tbsp. unrefined oil   *Flax oil*

    ¾ cup milk   *Soy milk*

    3 eggs separated

Preheat oven to 350°F.

Beat egg whites until stiff.

In a separate bowl beat egg yolks.

Add milk, oil and sugar to egg yolks.

Add dry ingredients and stir until smooth.

Gently fold in egg whites until batter is mixed.

Pour into an 8½" x 4¼" x 2½" loaf pan.

Bake until done.

HANNA KROEGER
PUBLICATIONS

Dear friends,

Many of the recipes presented in this book come to you from the kindness and inventiveness of people making the best of their misfortunes.

If you, too, have a favorite allergy baking recipe and would like to help lighten the load of your fellow man, feel free to send it with your name to me at 075 Valmont Road, Boulder, Colorado 80301.

I will be most happy to include your contributions with due credits in my next edition and you may be assured that each contribution will be treasured not only by me but by thankful people in many homes.

Thank you for your kindness and consideration.

Hanna Kroeger

I remain a friend who asked for help from others and now am sharing help others in need.

INDEX